Gardening at Night

By

Dottie Randazzo

Gardening at Night

by

Dottie Randazzo

Published by:

Creative Dreaming

6433 Topanga Cyn. Blvd.

Woodland Hills, CA 91303

All rights reserved. No part of this book may be reproduced or transmitted in any form or by any means, electronic or mechanical, including photocopying, recording or by any information storage and retrieval system, without permission from the author, except for the inclusion of brief quotations in a review.

Copyright © 2007 by Dottie Randazzo

ISBN 978-0-6151-8260-5

By Dottie Randazzo

Praying 101 for Spiritual Enlightenment
Praying 101 for Men
Praying 101 for Women
Praying 101 for Kids & Teens
Praying 101 for Parents

The Feeling
Trust
Are you a Spiritual Hypochondriac?

Introduction

You dream of living a different life. You desperately want your life to be different; however, change rocks your world.

If change rocks your world, how are you going to create the life you want, deserve and desire?

You can't change anything and keep it the same.

What you may dislike more than your routines are change.

Three definitions for "change" are:

    To make the form, nature, content, future course, etc., of (something) different from what it is or from what it would be if left alone.

    To transform or convert.

    To substitute another or others for; exchange for something else, usually of the same kind.

Those definitions don't sound bad to me. Yet, there are people who feel as if "change" is the kiss of death.

If you <u>feel</u> that way about change it will indeed <u>feel</u> that way to you.

Routines prevent change.

Routine has been defined as:

A customary or regular course of procedure.

Commonplace tasks, chores, or duties as must be done regularly or at specified intervals; typical or everyday activity.

Regular, unvarying habitual, unimaginative, or rote procedure.

An unvarying and constantly repeated formula, act of speech or action; convenient or predictable response.

A life should not be lived regular, unvarying, habitual, unimaginative or as a rote procedure.

Your life should be lived the same way it was when you were a small child. You should wake up each morning and be excited about the unforeseen changes and the unpredictability of life.

Know that each day a new window is being opened for you to experience the world and all of its wonders.

Change only rocks your world when you aren't open to anything different happening.

The ride on a roller coaster, with its ups and downs, twists and turns are like life. What you do on the ride or in your life determines how you *feel* about the ride or your life. If while on the roller coaster, you grip the arm rails white knuckled and tense up your body, it will not be a fun, pleasant, exciting ride. If you relax into the ride, not trying to resist the ups and downs and twists and turns, it can be a fun and exciting ride.

Living life is much like riding a roller coaster. **STOP HANGING ON.**

Stop being afraid. Your life is meant to be lived, not tucked away to be protected before it expires.

Making the transition from routine to change isn't one that

can be accomplished overnight; that would be too uncomfortable.

These pages contain numerous ways in which you can shift your energy and make change a part of your life. Read each suggestion. If it *feels* right, implement it into your life. The first change you implement will be the most uncomfortable as this is a new experience and *feeling* for you. When you *feel* comfortable, try another suggestion. This one will *feel* less uncomfortable as you are now becoming familiar with the feeling of change and it doesn't *feel* so foreign to you.

The more comfortable you *feel* regarding change, the more change can come into your life.

The change that will begin to come into your life will be the change that you will find necessary to create the life you truly want to live.

Eat dinner for breakfast and breakfast for dinner.

Change the way you feel about education.

Change your shoes.

Change your hair style or color.

Change the route you take to work.

Change where you eat your lunch.

Change what you do when you wake up in the middle of the night. If you normally read, then surf the internet. If you normally surf the internet, then read.

Change how you feel about volunteering.

Change what you listen to when commuting.

Change your exercise routine.

Change the way you react to negative news or information.

Change where you eat your dinner. If you normally eat at the dining room table, eat in another room. If you normally eat in another room, eat at the dining room table.

Change what you normally read. If you normally read beauty magazines, pick up a news magazine. If you normally read fiction, pick up a non-fiction book.

Change where you exercise.

Change your job.

Eat your salad last, instead of first.

Change the way you feel about poverty.

Change the pen you use to write with.

Change the length of time you spend in the shower or bath.

Rearrange or replace the pictures in your work environment.

If you normally take baths, change to showers. If you normally take showers, change to bath.

Change your makeup.

Change the time of day you pray or give thanks.

Change your purse.

Change when you groom your pet(s).

Change how you celebrate birthdays.

Change the time when you do your gardening or watering of your plants.

Change when you exercise.

Eat dessert first.

Change the way you feel about politicians.

Change where you eat your breakfast.

Change the time of
day you pay your bills.

Change the time you shower or bathe.

Change your hobby.

Rearrange or replace the pictures in your home environment.

Change the way you feel about strangers.

Change your socks.

Change the way you respond to people. If normally it is by phone, then send an email. If it is normally by email, then pick up the phone.

Write down all of the ways in which you would like to be different.

Change the way you give gifts. Instead of purchasing a gift, give something that you once owned. Or give the gift of washing someone's car, cleaning their home or walking their pet.

Change the way you say "Thank You."

Change the way you feel about the world.

Change the way you communicate with people. If you do more talking, start doing more listening. If you do more listening, start talking.

Change whom you would be friends with. If you only have thin friends, make friends with someone heavy. If you only have friends who are smarter than you, make friends with the garbage collector.

Change your underwear.

Rearrange your kitchen cabinets. Put the plates where you normally have the glasses and the glasses where you normally have the plates.

Change the way you feel about minorities.

Change the way you feel about your body image.

Change the way you spend time with your children.

Change the frames that your pictures are in.

Change the guilty thoughts you have about yourself.

Change your clock and/or the location of your clock.

Change your perception about life.

Change the way you feel about food and eating. If you are constantly thinking about how fattening something is, start thinking about how good it tastes.

Change the amount of time you spend in nature.

Change what you sing in the car or the shower. If you don't sing, then start singing.

Change the way you feel about people who are different than you.

Change the way you spend time with your family.

Change the pasta you normally eat. There are 150 different kinds to choose from.

Change how you greet people.

Change the light bulbs in your lamps.

Change the way you discipline your children.

Change the way you spend time with your friends. If you normally get together for dinner and movie, change it to snacks and a game.

Change the amount of time you spend walking.

Learn how to say hello, goodbye and/or thank you in another language.

Learn another language!

Change how you prepare your eggs.

Mix up your matching set of pillow cases and sheets on your bed.

Change the way you feel about yourself after you have made a mistake or bad choice.

Change the way you shop. If you only go into stores to shop, change and shop online. If you only shop online, change and go into the stores.

Change the way you discipline your pet(s).

Change how you handle a compliment.

Celebrate anything you want on any day you want.

Visit a church or spiritual organization that you normally would not.

Change your television viewing habits.

Prepare a turkey dinner in April.

Change how you argue.

Eat at a restaurant that you have never eaten.

Change your nail polish.

Do your holiday shopping in May, June or July.

Change the way you feel about spending money. Instead of being resentful after giving your money to the cashier, be grateful that you can provide an opportunity for him/her to be able to feed and clothe their families.

Change the coffee you drink.

Change the way you feel about illness.

Change your attitude.

Change your shampoo.

Change how you vacation. If you normally take land trips, change and take a cruise. If you normally take cruises, change and take a land trip.

Change the way you
feel about your life.

www.ingramcontent.com/pod-product-compliance
Lightning Source LLC
Chambersburg PA
CBHW032019040426
42448CB00006B/666